Read to Succeed:

How to Get Your Kids to Read

Read to Succeed:

How to Get Your Kids to Read

Martin Burley

First Printing: 2014 by Lulu Publishing
ISBN 978-1-291-90997-5

Dedication

To my amazing wife, Vicky, and fantastic children, Alfie and Daniel.
Your love and support has made the writing of this book possible.

CONTENTS

Author's Note   5
Introduction   10
Chapter 1: Read to Succeed   14
Chapter 2: Preparing Yourself   20
Chapter 3: The Conversation   25
Chapter 4: The Bedroom   33
Chapter 5: When and Where   36
Week 1   40
Week 2   47
Week 3   53
Week 4   57
Week 5   62
Week 6   66
Chapter 6: Happily Ever After   69
Chapter 7: The Revolution   72
Chapter 8: Phonics   75
Chapter 9: Guided Reading   80
Chapter 10: What to Read   84
Chapter 11: Reading at School   91
Afterword   94

AUTHOR'S NOTE

Firstly, let me be honest about the aims of this book.

I want to encourage you and your kids to read.

It may be that your child has fallen out of love with the written word (or were they never in love with books in the first place?), perhaps it's just that books have been usurped, overtaken and pushed to the back burner. Lots of people (teachers included) will shake their heads, tut and explain that your child should be 'reading for pleasure'. But this won't *just* happen; you have to convince your child that they need to 'read to succeed'.

In this book I lay out a simple, six week, step by step approach to get your child reading again.

I also want to be honest about what this book won't do.

It will not help you teach your kid to read. There are some hints about how to help struggling readers, but that's all. I don't want you buying this book under false pretences.

The advantages of regular reading are discussed further on, but I don't think anyone in their right mind really needs convincing of its benefits. So, if we can all agree that regular reading helps children then let's get more specific.

Who is this book actually aimed at?

Are you a parent or guardian of children aged between eight and sixteen? Then it could be you.

Do your children have an aversion to picking up a book, protest when made to read or claim reading is 'boring'? Then come in and settle down, we have much to discuss.

I hear these kinds of comments all the time in my day job as an English teacher and Literacy Coordinator. There is too much other stuff going on in kids' lives these days for them to just stop and read. Also, it's hard! Consider how intuitive computers, phones and tablets are these days: they do a lot of your thinking for you. When your child is fed a constant stream of information, without time to process and consider its relevance, you quickly realise they are losing a vital life skill. Because when you read, you're sharpening your brainpower – reading is to the mind what exercise is to the body.

I try hard in my job to encourage children to read, but I realised quite quickly that I am not the most important or influential person in their lives. You are. That's why I need your help.

But why listen to me? What makes me such an expert?

Well, the first thing is, I have never really considered myself an expert. I'm sorry if that doesn't inspire confidence, but to my mind it sounds a bit pompous.

However, in his book 'Outliers: The Story of Success', Malcolm Gladwell claims the key to success is applying the '10,000 Hour Rule' – to become an expert you need to take 10,000 hours of deliberate practice at something. If that's the case, then pompous or not, I do qualify.

I have worked as a teacher for over seven years and have always been involved in some area of Literacy. (Being an English teacher you would hope that was the case, wouldn't you?) So I believe I do have some ideas worth listening to.

I am not some kind of genius within this field, though. There are hundreds of people who understand the scientific theories behind Literacy and can write detailed articles on the subject. I'm not one of those people.

First and foremost, I am a father of two fantastic boys (at the time of writing aged thirteen and ten) who read widely and enjoy it. That's not to say they wouldn't rather be doing something else at times – they would, but we have an agreement. It doesn't *just* happen; a lot of work goes into it. But I'm convinced they 'read to succeed' and have been doing for years.

Secondly, as already stated, I am a teacher, so I understand the limitations of the school in encouraging your child to read. There is a lot to fit in during the school day, all the timetabled lessons, after school activities and pastoral care. Your child probably gets about three hours a week of English tuition – and their teacher will have to squeeze in an entire curriculum into that time. Hopefully they'll have a great and inspiring teacher, but I'm guessing that they'll be in a class with 30 other kids all demanding attention. So checking on your child's reading progress is not going to be at the forefront of their minds for the vast majority of the week. I'm sure they try, but there is only so much they can do. You might consider this a disgrace and complain they are not doing their job properly, but, to be honest, it's only masking the real issue – your kid doesn't read nearly as much as they should. That's why I'm here, to help you help yourselves.

Thirdly, I am a Literacy Coordinator. I do understand the importance of reading. I am fully aware of the obstacles that we all face to get youngsters reading. And, over the years, I have read widely and accessed lots of information about reading strategies.

But, perhaps most importantly, I haven't always been a teacher.

I think this is vitally important, so I'll apologise to my colleagues in the education field now, but I do know what life is like out in the 'real world'. I worked at a bank (as a customer facing cashier, not as an investment banker – so don't throw stones at me) for sixteen years. I know what it's like to get back home late, too tired to do anything except veg out in front of the telly, but with a hundred little jobs still to complete. The last thing I want to do is to make you feel guilty, like you're a bad parent. I'm guessing you may feel that already, because you're reading this book. Don't beat yourself up about the fact your child doesn't read – at least you've realised this and want to do something about it. You've made a step in the right direction – that's the sign of someone who cares about their children's future.

Finally, I am also a journalist and writer. That means I am used to communicating through the written word. I worked for an award-winning local magazine and wrote hundreds of articles for my local newspaper. I hope that means I can string a sentence together. And, gosh, if it's entertaining and informative as well, so much the better!

That's why I decided to write this book. I believe I have a few different hats I can wear at opportune moments to help you encourage your child to read. That's what we're both after, isn't it?

So, I've told you what this book can do and what it can't do. I've told you why I think I'm qualified to write it. Now, let's get to work.

INTRODUCTION

I'm going to start with an admission of guilt. If your children don't value reading, then I, as a teacher, can't change this on my own.

I'm sorry.

Ofsted may well denounce me as uninspiring and failing the children in my care. Whatever. I'm a realist. And my mum always told me to tell the truth.

I am always telling my students how to persuade their reader by using different writing techniques. I've just broken all the rules. That makes me a hypocrite as well.

Again, whatever.

Actually, I'm not here to persuade you that your kids need help in reading – you've picked this book up and I'm guessing that your ten year old daughter hasn't just finished reading 'The Hunger Games'. That's why you're here.

So, let's be honest. I have been. Now it's your turn.

Do you read?

'Well, I'm reading now, Mr Know-it-all,' you might be thinking. And great, but are your kids with you? Do they see you reading? Do you actually enjoy reading? Or, are you one of those parents that don't really do reading. It's not your cup of tea. You'll wait for the film to come out. You're too busy. You don't like make-believe stories, 'I'm not ten years old you know!'

Ok, I hear you. But all of these statements make it okay for your kid to dislike reading, they give them your permission not to read.

All of these anti-reading comments are like the sea washing over a rock-face. In time they grind down any enthusiasm – wear it away. They give 'not reading' the rubber stamp of acceptance. They give it legitimacy.

So that's the first thing you have to promise now. No more negative comments about reading. None. You have to catch your tongue when these comments start to form in your brain. These statements multiply before they reach your kids' ears. (There you go: I've thrown in that mathematical term for my numerical friends)

No fingers crossed behind your back - I can see you. You have to be positive.

Or, if you can't quite find the motivation to be positive, at least don't be negative. Promise?

There are loads of books out there that will tell you why reading is crucial to your child's career chances. They will quote lots of statistics, cite relevant case studies and pepper their books with so called, 'motivational quotes'. But, I'm not going to do that.

I could just play the teacher card and answer the question, 'Why is reading important?' with, 'Just because it is!' But that's just passing the buck (pardon the pun) isn't it?

Reading opens doors.

That's about the size of it really. The more you read, the more you will know, the better your vocabulary will be, the more intelligent you will sound, the more you will impress the people who determine your future. Simple as that.

Think of reading as your child's key to their future. It unlocks their potential.

But reading isn't easy these days. There are lots of other distractions that seem much more interesting and immediately satisfying. My boys are like that too – X-Box, Nintendo 3DS, Samsung Galaxy Tablets, as well as their laptops. Whisper this, but even I can be found scrolling down my Twitter feed on my i-pad. If your child is a teenager then they'll have the same problems: Facebook, Instagram and Snapchats. Everything in life is at their fingertips and they respond within seconds to a message from their friends. How can reading match the excitement of that?

It won't be easy. But it can be done. It may take all your parenting skills, the patience of a saint and the diplomacy of a bureaucrat, but it is a war we have to win – for their sakes. Any prospective employer won't be wooed by someone who is adept at gossiping on Facebook or who can shorten everything they do into 140 characters.

Reading is never going to be cool - unless your kid is a bookworm. And, once again, that's not why you're reading this is it?

So a little bit of strategy is going to be required in re-engaging your child with reading. They might not be 'reading for pleasure' in a few weeks, but, as I discuss later, as long as they 'read to succeed' we're on the right track. Tweeting the fact they've just finished a Dickens classic may prove a step too far, or letting slip their feelings on Heathcliff's relationship in Wuthering Heights whilst chatting to their pals. But if, in time, they do have opinions like this that they keep to themselves, well, we'll just have to settle for that, won't we?

So, over the next few chapters I'm going to try and help you set up a regime that will help your child re-discover their inner bookworm. Some of this may work well, other ideas may not be for you. It may turn them into a book-a-week child, it may just help them read a little more often. As long as there is a win – even a little one – then your child's opportunities in life will have been improved.

CHAPTER ONE:

READ TO SUCCEED

Pleasure is defined as being a feeling of happy satisfaction and enjoyment.

This is why I have a real problem with 'reading for pleasure' - one of the widely used phrases supposed to convince reluctant readers to engage with books.

Now, 'reading for pleasure' is something I do often - my wife, and even my children do it too – they all enjoy reading books. A great story can bring a smile to their face, make them cry or, sometimes, even scare them rigid. At some point it will create an emotion strong enough to encourage them to continue turning that page.

However, telling someone who doesn't like reading that it will give them pleasure (remember: leave them happily satisfied) is like trying to tell a nine year old boy that he will enjoy broccoli.

It just won't happen.

You might get him to eat it by explaining how much good it will do him and persuading him of its 'super veg' qualities, but enjoyment? That's only going to happen some distance down the road.

Lots of people out there list gardening as one of their favourite hobbies. They love pottering about, deadheading flowers and cultivating plants. Not me. I don't like gardening. If I could concrete over the garden and paint it green, I'd be a happy man.

However I do see the benefits of gardening; I like sitting in the garden on a nice day (reading a good book) or playing cricket with my sons. I appreciate that flowers can look attractive and that home-grown vegetables taste better than their shop bought equivalent. I get it, I really do.

So I garden. But I don't enjoy it. It's not pleasurable – it's a chore.

So when a kid tells me they don't like reading, I try to imagine what that must be like. I think of how I feel about gardening. And if someone told me to 'garden for pleasure' I'd be likely to tell them where to stick their spades and rakes.

That's why I think 'reading for pleasure' is completely the wrong way to go about encouraging a child to read. Hopefully they will enjoy it eventually, but it won't come easy and it doesn't happen quickly.

So, I want to try a new approach I have labelled 'read to succeed'. This accepts that your child may not like reading; it doesn't promise things it can't deliver. It is a simple acknowledgement that the more your kid reads, the greater their chance to succeed.

The skills your child will develop from reading can be linked mnemonic style to this:

S – Scheme

U – Understand

C – Communicate

C – Create

E – Empathise

E – Enquire

D – Discover

Reading helps develop all of these skills. If you can convince your child of the benefits of improving these, then it might be an easier sell than simple enjoyment.

Let's have a look at why each of these skills will help your child to succeed.

Read to Scheme – this might seem a little odd at first. Scheming certainly does have negative connotations. It can conjure up an image of someone plotting against you or coming up with plans to trip you up. But when you consider the cunning required in plotting and planning effectively, hopefully you will be able to see the benefit. 'Reading to scheme' allows your child to grow their strategic thinking skills, to look ahead and see how things might develop, allowing them to plan accordingly. It's an invaluable talent to possess.

Read to Understand – I shouldn't need to explain this one in any great depth. You need to be able to understand texts that are placed in front of you. If you can work out the true meaning of a text then you'll be able to make a much more informed decision on how to respond. Understanding texts gets easier the more you read. Simples.

Read to Communicate – hopefully you have a good relationship with your child and your conversations do actually consist of a few spoken, articulate words: not just grunts. I'm sure that you want them to be able to conduct a lucid discussion when they are older. Reading is all about communication – allowing someone to pass information to thousands of people by writing stuff down. Reading widely will increase your child's word power and show them how to communicate effectively.

Read to Create – to be a good writer, you must read a lot. I heard that first from legendary horror author, Stephen King, and it still holds true. If you have some good ideas (you don't need to be writing a best-selling novel, it can be any kind of creative thought) then reading will help you to develop these into something more tangible. And if you do want to improve your writing skills then modelling your skills on your favourite author is something all top writers have done at some point or another. Reading gives you the thinking skills that allow you to create and imagine.

Read to Empathise – citizenship was a buzz word in education a few years ago. But I feel it is still vitally important today. The one thing I want for my children is for them to grow up into responsible adults ready to make a contribution to the world. Empathy is a critical skill in this regard. Being able to put yourself into the shoes of someone else and understand what they are going through is a vital, global, social requirement. Reading books and empathising with characters allows your child to practise this skill in a safe environment.

Read to Enquire – I don't want your child to accept as gospel, everything they are told (unless of course it's one of those times when you just need to invoke the power of 'because I say so'). Hopefully you'll want them to question and investigate things for themselves. An enquiring mind is something that will stand them in good stead as they move through life, making good decisions on who to believe and who to interrogate further.

Read to Discover – your child may discover they enjoy reading. This may lead them to 'reading for pleasure' fairly quickly, but it's probably not something they will adapt to instantly. Every child needs to find that certain book or story that takes them to a different place, that completely engulfs them and teaches them something they had never thought of before. Discovery is one of the most beneficial learning experiences a child can have. You can tell them things a thousand times, until you are blue in the face (I have plenty of experience of that), but when you can let them discover it for themselves – well, that's something they'll remember for the rest of their lives.

If all of these skills can be developed through reading; if your child becomes adept at scheming, understanding, communicating, creating, empathising, enquiring and discovering – well, I'll be happy. I'd pretty much guarantee their lives will be more successful as a result.

CHAPTER TWO:

PREPARING YOURSELF

One thing can be absolutely guaranteed. If you don't change, neither will your child.

There is one person in this room that has the biggest effect on your child's willingness and desire to read, and that's you.

Not me. Not their English teacher. You.

You are the person they have looked up to all of their lives. It may not feel that way at the moment, particularly if teenage hormones have surfaced, but it's true.

So, before we start looking at how to develop our six week reading programme, you need to take a look at your own reading habits. You've made a good start – you're reading now. But if your child spots you leafing through this book they will know you have an ulterior motive. I've tried to keep this book brief. It could well fit quite easily in-between the pages of a best-selling hardback. I'm not suggesting that this book should be hidden away like a dirty magazine, but reading it out of your child's view has to be the way forward. If your kid gets a sniff of what we're trying to achieve here then it will be doubly difficult to get them reading. They can be quite stubborn, kids.

Now, you may be an avid reader. You may be frustrated at your kid's lack of interest in the books you love. But remember, just because you can't wait to find out how Darcy and Elizabeth end up in 'Pride and Prejudice' doesn't mean that a Jane Austen classic is going to float their boat. They need to be able to find their own stories, perhaps ones that speak to them in a more modern voice.

So pushing lots of different book choices at them isn't going to work. You need to be a bit more open-minded about the whole process.

Conversely, you may not be a big fan of reading. This may be because of the distractions I mentioned earlier, or because you have difficulty reading yourself.

No matter.

The first step to getting your kids to read is to model reading. That doesn't mean you have to walk up and down your living room with a dog-eared copy of 'Twilight' in your hand, working it, baby.

No, it means you have to be caught reading.

This is an absolutely critical point. Not seen reading – caught.

You know what time your kid traipses in through the door from school, or walks in at the weekend treating your home like a hotel room. Well, ten minutes before they come in, make yourself a cup of tea, turn off the TV (who can watch 'Deal or No Deal' everyday anyway) and any other mobile devices (or at least put them on silent and ignore them for a while). Pick up a book, any book will do, except one aimed at their age group – they will see that as far too obvious and embarrassing. Try and think of one that might even surprise them, one you might even feel self-conscious reading yourself. What the hell, go '50 Shades of Grey' if you feel daring.

Then read.

You'll hear them arrive. Bang the door behind them. Perhaps grunt at you or demand to be fed and watered. So, what you do next is critical – ignore them. Yes, you heard right – ignore them. Let's face it, they've done it to you often enough so why not give them a little payback. Just don't give in when they start yawping for your help – make sure you look completely engrossed in your book.

Let *them* come and find out where you are and what you're doing. When they do see you, there are a couple of options you can take. Either feign embarrassment and quickly put the book down hiding it somewhere they can't see it – intrigue them. Or, carry on ignoring them – show them you are so absorbed in the book you're reading that everything else pales into insignificance until they finally ask you, 'What are you reading that's so damn interesting?'

That's the first question we need them to ask. Once that's achieved you're on the downward slope. They've seen how a book can completely captivate you and capture your imagination.

You need to start this procedure at least a couple of months before we actually begin the six week challenge of getting your kid to read. Because then we can start and embed the idea of reading into their heads before we actually broach the subject.

Now, things may move faster than I outline in this book. If you have a really good relationship with your kid they may want to read the book they caught you so interested in. Well, great – go for it. You may not even have to wait and complete the entire challenge. If the end product is the same then how we get there matters little. They're reading, their imagination has been fired, and their career prospects have been enhanced.

But if this seems to have been only of momentary interest to them, if they actually ask the question and lose interest in your reply, then we still have work to do.

Reading, and being caught reading, must then be something that happens on a regular basis. Don't ever question them about it or wave it in their face, let them see your new habit. If possible, engage the rest of the family in the project. Talk about a book with your partner, or parent, or friend – it doesn't matter who. But let them catch you talking about it. Open the conversation as you hear them coming down the stairs or when you know they are about to enter the room. Don't talk to them – let them overhear you.

This is all part of the groundwork required for your project.

If you are au fait with social media then you could even employ this as part of your overall strategy. Join a Facebook group that has a fan site of the book you're reading. If your kid actually follows you on Twitter, then tweet about how you're enjoying the book – if you can get someone to reply to you then so much the better.

You know your child will read this, but, as far as they know, it's not aimed at them.

During this time your kid might even ask you what it is want for your birthday/ Christmas/Mother's Day etc. This gives you a great opportunity to ask for a book – not to interrogate them about why they don't read, but to show that you do – and you don't care who knows.

So now you're almost ready. You have opened your own eyes to reading, or re-discovered the joy of following a character through a few hundred pages. You have been positive about the act of reading and shown to your child that this is a pastime you enjoy and is worthwhile.

Take a deep breath – it's time to start the six week challenge.

CHAPTER THREE:

THE CONVERSATION

The first part of the challenge may actually prove to be the hardest: you need to have 'the conversation'.

Yes, actually sitting your child down, free of distractions, and talking to them is never the easiest task. When you ask for a talk, make clear the gravity of the situation and how serious the issue is that you need to discuss. Don't leap into the talk, arrange a time and let them stew over the possibilities for a little while. Remember, don't tell them it's about reading.

The chances are that when they finally discover that you want to discuss reading (and not the birds and the bees) they will be quite relieved and agree to give the six week challenge a try.

Because the key word here is 'agree'.

Think of this as an anti-addiction. It is commonly acknowledged that all addicts must want to help themselves before any kind of resolution of their issues can be achieved. The same goes for 'not reading'. Your kids need to see how this will benefit them, how reading will help them succeed in the future, even if they are wary of the journey they need to take to get there.

So, how should this conversation go?

Make sure you've told them you need a chat. You might have carved out some time between Call of Duty assignments, or waited until they are in bed. Whatever. You know the best time to talk to your child, preferably free of digital distractions.

Now, I don't want to appear arrogant and teach you how to talk your own offspring – I'm hoping that you'll know best how to approach this delicate issue. However, I've put together a structure that you may find helpful. Remember that one of the key skills that reading helps develop is 'how to scheme'. By following this kind of format you will hopefully arrive at the desired outcome:

1) Talk about their latest school report/results/assessment. The chances are that if you need to implement the strategies in this book then your child's progress is not what either of you are hoping for. They may be falling behind in any subject; it doesn't have to be just English.

For any pupil to access the National Curriculum they must have a reading age of at least nine years and six months. Sounds low, doesn't it? Surely your child is above this?

Well, I hope so, but you may be surprised. Does your child's school even know what their current reading age is? A lot won't.

And even if your child's reading age is higher than nine and a half, but below their chronological age, then they are still walking into every single classroom at a disadvantage before the lesson even begins. I'm positive you don't want that to happen.

They may not see this as a big issue. The overwhelming majority of children I've come across want to keep any sign of underachievement from their parents. Whether this is because they'll get in trouble, or feel as though they are a disappointment to you, doesn't matter. They don't want to tell you and they won't want to talk about it.

So you will have to remain focused on the outcome. Don't get led down any dark allies or get side-tracked about who they have been forced to sit next to, or how the teacher hates them, or that the teacher doesn't know what they are doing. Some of these things may be true, but they are outside your realm of influence.

Focus on the fact that things aren't good enough and that they need to make a change.

Use their excuses positively. If they become distracted in school then by making a change outside of school they could resolve the problem. If their teacher doesn't know what they are doing, then they need to take responsibility to ensure they are not held back by this.

Agree that small changes need to be made.

2) Talk about how reading is the biggest single activity they can get involved in to improve their grades.

I told you I wasn't going to bombard you with facts and statistics about reading – and I meant it. But you need to get this message across.

Reading is the single biggest indicator for social mobility.

That means the more your child reads, the more successful they are likely to become – increasing their chances of getting a better job.

According to surveys completed by the National Literacy Trust reading has a bigger impact than anything else, including your social class.

Reading helps develop many critical thinking skills. If your kid agrees that they need to improve their school performance then pitch this as an easy solution. Not only will it help them develop, but it will also stop you constantly getting on their back.

You could try and suggest some more unpalatable alternatives first. Ask them if they need extra tutoring, if they want to get involved in after school catch-up sessions or if they need extra homework? There aren't many kids I know who would volunteer for these options.

Agree to read, tell them, and the rest remains on the back burner – and, do you know what else? You get to pick what you read.

3) Hopefully now you'll have agreement that reading is the way forward. Is now the time to hammer that home with a contract? If you want to be very organised and like agreements in triplicate then, by all means, write it down. However, a verbal agreement is just as good – hopefully it also shows some degree of trust.

The agreement must be that they will read for at least fifteen minutes every day for one week.

After that week you'll meet up again – same bat time, same bat channel – and re-assess.

The book they read is up to them.

There are just a few provisos:

- They must not have read the book, or any part of it before.
- It must be a fiction book at this stage (this just removes arguments about the Guinness Book of Records and the like).
- It must be a book that they have not seen the film of.
- And most importantly, they must have all electronic devices turned off.

(A little word here about electronic devices. Many people read on them quite successfully and, if you have a basic Kindle or e-reader, then they could be used instead of a regular book. However if you have an app on an i-pad, things won't go as planned. With the best will in the world your child will become distracted by checking their Twitter account or some other social media site.

Pitch it to them like this: turning your electronic device off for 15 minutes won't kill you, it won't mean that your friends will fall out with you and it won't ruin your social life. In fact, when you turn on the device again you will feel extremely popular, because you'll have 15 minutes of your Twitter feed to catch up on. Embrace it – it will be liberating.)

4) Incentives. Kids these days always seem to need one before they'll actually get anything done. Will this set them up adequately for life outside the classroom? I'm not sure. But it is something they are used to. You may have already done something similar before – perhaps with a sticker chart on the fridge if they went to bed on time, or bought them a new x-box game if they did well in their school report.

There is one great incentive you can use here that also has a learning element to it. (We love stuff like that, us teachers.) When your child selects a book, tell them to pick one that has been made into a film. There are loads to choose from – and some great movies at that. At the time of writing The Hunger Games movies are extremely popular. This year we've had Beautiful Creatures and The Hobbit.

Select a film they haven't seen (remember that rule from earlier on – it's really important) and agree a deal with them. When they've finished the book then you'll have a big family film night. You could rent the DVD, buy the movie from Sky or wherever and settle down one Saturday night to watch it.

Now, it depends on how big an incentive you are prepared to give them or can afford, but you could order in pizza, buy that family sized bag of Doritos or indulge in your favourite chocolate snacks. But make a night of it.

'But what about that learning point?' I hear you ask.

Well, it all stems from an event we had in school. We read a Michael Morpurgo book (great author, any of his books would work fine) called Private Peaceful. The kids don't seem to mind being read to in class (I suppose it beats writing) and they really like the characters in this World War One tale. When we had read the book we got the whole year group in the hall and let them watch the film. (Before putting them into groups and doing some collaborative work on the book – I don't want to give the impression we just watch movies without any purpose.)

After it had finished I couldn't get over the comments that they made. Virtually all of them complained about how the movie had missed particular elements of the story out. They didn't cover this and they brushed over that – they were quite beside themselves.

This is why it is of vital importance you don't watch a film before reading the book. If you watch the film after, although enjoyable, the chances are that some of your favourite bits are still on the cutting room floor. Films are only 90 minutes long; they simply haven't the time to cover all the nuances of a story.

Fingers crossed your child will respond in the same way and talk about what the movie didn't show. It's quite an easy step to talk about how books are better than movies from that standpoint.

5) Reinforcement. Finally you need to talk about how you make this happen. Don't be wishy-washy at this stage and allow your kid to just say, 'Yeah, I'll grab 15 minutes at some point over the day.' You've come this far, stick to your guns.

Nail down when and where this will happen. Is it going to be as soon as they come in from school, so they can do it and know the rest of the evening is their own? Or will it be bedtime, when they are tucked in nice and warm? You have the option here to extend lights out by 15 minutes as long as they are reading – might that be another incentive?

So, conversation over, strategy deployed – now is the time to let the magic happen.

CHAPTER FOUR:

THE BEDROOM

Right, I don't want to come over all teacher-preachy. So I'll apologise here and now if that happens, because it might.

I hate it when I visit my children's schools on parent's evening and feel as though some young girl straight out of teacher training college who hasn't even had a boyfriend yet, (let alone thought about starting a family) is looking down her snooty nose at the way I choose to bring up my boys. But there are some fundamental principles I have always believed in when it comes to raising children and I need to share them with you.

When I was a kid I never had a TV in my room. You might think I was a deprived child, but it never really bothered me. I know that when I got married my wife wanted a TV she could watch while curled up under the duvet. But I was never keen – I always thought bedtime was for sleeping and other grown-up activities, not for catching up with Coronation Street. So this was something I followed through when we had our boys.

I actually think this is more important now than at any other point in our lifetimes. The TV in my wife's room when she was a kid played four channels. There was no VCR or Catch-Up TV which meant you could watch anything you wanted. There was no DVD player so she could watch Dirty Dancing or Grease till silly o'clock. There was no Game Boy or Nintendo DS you could take under the covers with you and irreparably damage your eyesight with. There was no mobile phone you could text message your friends with until you fell asleep. There was no games console that allowed you to play with your friends till the early hours of the morning, making you so tired that you caught up with your nap during Chemistry. There was no laptop that invited God-knows who directly into your bedroom with one click of a mouse. There was no tablet computer spurting out vile pornography and teaching you all the wrong messages on how to conduct a loving relationship.

In our house my kids have access to all these gadgets, but they do so in the living room. Granted this can be a pain while we're trying to watch the next episode of Homeland and some Minecraft parody is playing along in the background. But I know they're safe. And I also know that when they go to bed they will read – there's nothing else for them to do.

So, while not wanting to preach, I would recommend removing electronic gadgets from their rooms. It will be liberating – for them as well as you.

Try and give them access to a bookcase – even a little shelf – somewhere in their room, so they can keep their favourite books on it. It makes the room look like someone reasonably intelligent resides there. It also means that their favourite books are readily available to them in idle moments.

My youngest son loves Diary of a Wimpy Kid and the Tom Gates books (both thoroughly recommended) and keeps them in his room. He's always re-reading his favourite parts. Often, when he has finished reading his school book, and still has a few minutes of reading time left before lights out, he'll grab a copy and chuckle along to the amusing bits.

Actually, I have to give a bit of a shout out to our school library for the discovery of Liz Pichon's Tom Gates series. I work closely with our Librarian and he came in with the first two of the series he'd found on offer in a book store at the weekend. I took them home so my youngest could try them out and (whisper this so I don't get fined) he still has them now.

If you have the space then you could try and create a little reading area with (if you have the money) some cool furniture that can be lazed around on while catching up with the latest developments in their book. These break-out areas have proved quite effective in our school, making reading just that little bit more inviting than cold classrooms, hard chairs and an absolute clinical silence.

So, I'm not talking about making your child's bedroom a prison cell, just somewhere they can be comfortable and focused on reading. And, in my opinion, that's best done without electronic distractions. Call me old-fashioned if you like – but it definitely works.

CHAPTER FIVE:

WHEN AND WHERE

Your child may well ask, 'When can I read?'

The easy answer is to say, 'Whenever you can.'

But this is not really an answer. Scheduling in time is vitally important and there is not a one size fits all response to this.

Reading before bedtime is great. It has many advantages as it can allow extra time before 'lights out' which can often be an incentive to those reluctant readers. There is no rush to complete reading as, when your child has finished, it will be time to go to sleep. It really is a great settling activity as well – you might not think that this is important to slightly older children, but I'd beg to differ. Even at my age I sleep better if I wind down with a good book before bedtime.

The downsides are that a scary book can give nightmares. My eldest son certainly suffered from this when he attempted to read the Twilight series of books. He woke up regularly one week petrified, as he was being chased by wolf-like animals. We quickly twigged that this was probably related to the book and swapped it for something a little less frightening. I would say that mild nightmares ought not to be feared and show a vivid imagination – but we have your well-being and sleep to consider as well. No-one likes to be awakened by a screaming kid in the early hours of the morning.

Other difficulties can include a child falling to sleep while reading or losing concentration. Also, if there is a special event on the TV, or a family party, then this time suddenly becomes squeezed out quite quickly. It is imperative that, if this is the agreed time, that allowances are made for these variables: for instance, ensuring they read earlier that day.

Some children may be more alert straight from school and want to get their reading 'out of the way'. This attitude is to be discouraged if at all possible, certainly as time goes on. Your child may not find it easy to be positive immediately. Obviously you should always be alert to this and take any opportunity of positive reinforcement – by this I mean that if your child over runs their allotted time, even by a few minutes, then comments relating to 'how interesting the book must be' can be made.

The main issue with timing is that of rushing to complete reading, so something else can be done instead (normally going outside in the summer, or playing on the computer if it's cold). That's why it's important to establish a time limit rather than a page count. Fifteen pages can be ghosted over fairly rapidly, while fifteen minutes is, and always has been, fifteen minutes.

Other strategies that can be used here is to bring them a cup of tea a minute or two before they finish, which often has the effect of extending reading time until the cup has been drained. Try and sit and chat to them after reading if possible – just take the opportunity to engage with each other.

And remember – all electronic devices should be off!

'Where' is just as important. In the living room while you're watching 'The Chase' is never going to work. Some children will talk about multi-tasking and their ability to pay attention whilst talking. Take it from me, if a child is talking and interested in the conversation, they won't be paying attention to what they are reading. So it needs to be some place quiet.

Their bedroom would work fine, but if you have an area where you normally work, a study or something similar, then this might work just as well, if not better. Allowing them access to space they don't often get to use is another sub-conscious tick in the 'importance of reading' column. It makes them realise how important this activity really is – reading to succeed.

Comfortable would be good as well. In the summer an attractive spot in the sun would work, or a cosy spot in an old, favourite armchair in the winter. It shouldn't be seen as some kind of homework chore to complete on a hard chair at the kitchen table, it should be a relaxing experience.

One of the key difficulties many children find with reading is their inability to concentrate on one thing for a specified length of time. Children are so used to being stimulated by their electronic devices or during lessons at school (the amount of 'episodes' we are encouraged to use in one lesson is evidence of this as no-one wants the little darlings to become bored for more than a minute) they can become fidgety and distracted.

Concentration is a key life skill and shouldn't be seen in a negative light. If your child can sit and read without interruption for quarter of an hour, then this is definitely a positive point to take away. In the world of work we all know that having to concentrate on the task in hand is a vital skill we need at regular points in our lives.

But having a regular time and place is absolutely essential. It becomes a habit – and that's exactly what we are after, for reading to become something they do, all the time.

If they can 'read to succeed' now – then 'reading for pleasure' might be something they learn to do for the rest of their lives.

WEEK ONE

So, (in the words of Shelter, a character from another thoroughly recommended book, Stone Cold) your planning has been meticulous and your preparations are complete.

But if I can extend the metaphor a little further: the ground work has been done, the foundations dug and now it's time to start building your child's imagination through reading.

You have reached agreement over the details (sweated the small stuff) and now is the time to follow through your plans. Now is the time for you to show your strength.

The book your child will be reading should be in place. If you can make it a new copy, then do so. There is something about an unbroken spine and the smell of a new book that heightens the excitement – it does in me anyway.

If, at this late stage, you are still unsure of which text to pick then check out the recommended reading lists at the back of this book.

The time and place should be sorted.

This is where you need to show support. But you need to do it covertly – not in a sly or underhand sense – just not in an overly obvious fashion. Standing over your child ensuring they read is the quickest way to ensure failure of this project. You need to show an element of trust.

One critical piece of equipment you should have is a bookmark. This will tell you quite a lot about the extent of your child's reading – hopefully they won't be so underhand as to move the bookmark a few pages every night. It allows you to see how progress is being made through the text.

Leave them the 15 minutes you agreed when you had the 'conversation' and don't interrupt them (apart from that cup of tea a couple of minutes before they finish). Ensure that mobile devices are turned off and there are no distractions. It might be a good idea if every electronic piece of equipment in the house was turned off. Sometimes the distant sound of the Coronation Street theme tune can be more off-putting than having a blaring TV in your room. It will also give you the opportunity to have a read of something yourself, in fact it could be the right moment for the entire family to take the chance to read. My sons and I have just started reading 'The Emerald Atlas' by John Stephens (even though my eldest son has read it before). We all sit together and take turns in reading a paragraph each. It is a great way for younger readers to hear how certain words and phrases should be read.

After the time is over congratulate your child, tell them how pleased you are that they are making such an effort to improve their reading skills. Don't ask them if they enjoyed it, or what happened in the book. They may volunteer this information – wait for that moment when they do, otherwise you may come across as being controlling.

The most important aspect is to ensure that this happens every night for the first week.

At some point in the future, when your kid turns out to be a voracious reader and is devouring books left, right and centre, there are going to be times when they miss a couple of nights or take a bit of a break between books.

Now is definitely not the time to allow this to happen.

During the week there will be something that comes up to potentially stop this reading session. It may be a weekly sports engagement, an impromptu party or a vital conversation with their mate. Whatever it is their reading has to be managed as part of this. You may need to bring the reading time forward or push it back. Remember, bedtime can be delayed to ensure that this is completed.

Don't fall into the trap of allowing them to double up the time the following day. This rarely happens! Once a reading session is missed in these early stages it is the beginning of the slippery slope to failure.

So, be strong. Make the reading happen – success depends upon it.

At the end of the first week when all seven sessions have been completed your child will have read for almost two hours. On average, most people will read about 50 pages an hour – this should mean they will be 80-90 pages through the book. For a lot of books, and I'm assuming you haven't selected 'War and Peace' as their re-introduction to reading, 200-300 pages is not an uncommon length. So they could almost be halfway through their book. Check their bookmark – does this look about right?

If you want to check their bookmark on a more regular basis (I'm not saying you should snoop on your kids, but sometimes you need to snoop on your kids) then between 10-15 pages a night would seem about right.

When you had your first conversation you should have scheduled in another quick chat at the end of the first week just to see how things are going. This isn't so you can berate them or interrogate them about events in the book – just to see how things are going.

At this stage you may feel things are fine and can continue as they are into Week 2. If your kid is showing signs of engagement and enjoyment then perhaps you can extend the time to 20 minutes, or add an extra session of 15 minutes at some point over the weekend.

The difficulties arise if there is some resistance to the plan. So, what may have gone wrong?

Your child may be quite willing to read, but just hasn't found the time to do so. They have perhaps missed a couple of sessions, because of one reason or another. This means that, in all likelihood, the trial will grind slowly to a halt. Two missed sessions will become three; your child will forget what is happening in their book and disengage with the characters. If they are not regular readers (and let's face it, if they were you wouldn't have got this far) then their ability to retain information may not be great. It is imperative that they read regularly.

In this case you need to look again at your plan and be stricter about allocating the necessary time for reading. Stress to your child that the outcome you are both after will not happen unless the reading sessions are an absolute priority. Remember about those unpalatable alternatives we mentioned – after school sessions or extra homework? A gentle reminder of these may be all that is required to steer your child back on course.

It may be that they are struggling with the book you have given them. Many people are tempted to saddle their kid with a classic and expect them to understand the nuances surrounding a Bronte or an Austen. You need to be realistic with your book choice, particularly at the start. You need a book they will enjoy, understand and finish. If it does not meet these requirements then your child is being set up to fail. So if it is a book choice issue then be flexible and change it if required. The whole issue here is that they 'read to succeed'. I understand that we are imposing certain aspects, but forcing your child to read a book they really don't like is never going to give us a positive outcome.

Your child may not be as good a reader as you think they are. The book may be perfectly enjoyable, but, due to a lack of experience, your child may just not be able to understand what is going on. If this is the case then we have a few deeper issues to address. We may need to go back to the drawing board look at how your child de-codes words and reads to the punctuation. This book is designed to help reluctant readers and so I don't want to get bogged down in the science of Literacy here, but you may need to try and sit with your child and help them read their book. This actually has a lot of benefits. It means taking a much more hands-on approach to the whole business. Sitting with your child and taking it in turns to read a page or a paragraph at a time may seem like an immature activity to partake in, but as I've just mentioned, it's actually a lot of fun and can be a great learning activity. If you're still really struggling then check out the sections at the back of the book on Phonics and Guided Reading.

There may be a more deep seated resentment to reading. I'm guessing that if this were truly the case then you wouldn't have reached this point – you'd still be trying to prepare the ground and have 'The Conversation'. But there is a chance that it is only when the actual reading takes place that the real antipathy kicks in. Again, more work is needed here. Is it really reading that is the issue, or is it more to do with concentration levels? Perhaps you could take things a bit slower and reduce reading time by 5 minutes a session before building it up more gradually. You can help your child here by taking opportunities to allow them to concentrate on particular tasks. If they are struggling with something, gently point out their attachment to their mobile, laptop, tablet (delete as appropriate). If they can

n end staring at the latest x-box game then
ould point out that their attention span is a little
atever the issue, you need to delve down to the
roblem.

Once you have highlighted the real issue and talked through a solution you need to make a decision on how best to proceed. Don't worry about repeating this week – there's no rush. It doesn't matter if the whole process takes six weeks or six months. All we want is a positive outcome.

Now, if you're ready, we'll move onto Week Two.

WEEK TWO

Now the time has come to up your game. If this week has gone well you can expect your child to be 150 pages or more into the new book they have been reading. This should be at least halfway through if not more. Hopefully there will be some sense of engagement with the characters and the plotline. You may not know yet; it depends very much on whether your kid has actually spoken to you about the book.

If you are experiencing any of the problems mentioned in the last chapter then you should go back and try to resolve these issues, even if it means taking a step back in the programme – Rome wasn't built in a day.

It might be worth mentioning at this point that even if you have to go back this is still something you can't afford to let rest. It's so easy to take the path of least resistance, the easy option. I know from my experiences in the classroom that kids will do pretty much anything to get out of doing something remotely difficult. Even if that means moaning at you until you give up. Well I'm going to moan at you as well – DON'T GIVE UP!

Remember who the adult is in this relationship. These days it appears that many parents are obsessed with being friends with their offspring. And you can be, most of the time: but you are a parent first. Don't feel I'm criticizing if this describes your relationship – lots of teachers get confused as well. But you have to come to terms with the fact that you are guiding your kid through childhood – hopefully most of the time they'll love you, but you have to accept that on occasion you will have to be the grown up, the bad guy. This does involve saying 'no'. I know it's not easy to refuse your child something or disappoint them, but you have a moral responsibility to be the adult and sometimes that means you know what's best.

Think about how much reading will benefit your child's future. It may not seem important now, but this is the biggest single thing you can do to help your children succeed. An improved vocabulary is vital for them to compete with other kids in the job market. Being able to work out what is being asked of you in written communication is critical in most workplaces these days. And being well read will improve their emotional intelligence no end.

Anyway, so Week Two is now complete. You have checked the movement of bookmark, perhaps even extended the number of reading sessions that your child has to complete. Everything is going well.

One of the key skills to reading is understanding. This is where some kids are now struggling, as they were taught to read using Phonics. Don't get me wrong, this is a great way of learning to de-code text and recognise the sounds that words are made up of. However, it does not help you to decipher the meaning of texts and work out what is being implied. This is of vital importance in every subject at secondary school – it is called inference.

Being able to work out what is being inferred is a skill all children need to possess. I could tell you that Charlie, at the back of the class wasn't paying attention – and you'd know exactly what I meant. It wouldn't tax your brain at all and, to be honest, if a book was telling you this all the time it'd get dreadfully dull. Or, I could say, 'Charlie gazed longingly out of the window, his teacher's voice becoming ever distant as he imagined himself out there, scoring the winning goal in the school's important cup final'. Suddenly you know Charlie isn't paying attention – I didn't tell you this outright. I implied it, you inferred it.

But you also know a lot more besides. Charlie might just be an idle good-for-nothing layabout, but he might also be an intelligent, normally attentive student – it's just that today he has something else on his mind.

When we write like this, we call it 'showing not telling' and it helps us develop an important reading skill: to be able to read between the lines.

Just imagine the mood and tone of an e-mail from your boss asking you to do something you don't want to do. If the tone implies it's important to do it, you might think twice and infer that this is vital for your career prospects. If you don't have this skill, if you have never read and worked things out for yourselves, this e-mail might not be deemed important, and end up costing you your job.

But why am I telling you all this?

It is because the next part of the programme involves you trying to improve your child's skill in this area.

Now, if you feel this is too soon and that while things are going well you'd rather not rock the boat, then delay it. That's cool – this is not a plan carved in stone - everyone's an individual. If your child needs more time then let them have it. You might want them to finish the first book before you introduce other exercises into the arena. No worries.

But as I am basing this around a six week plan it would be prudent of me to introduce these extra skills around now. I want to try and give you an exercise that your child can complete at the end of every week from now until the end of the programme. These exercises have been carefully devised to try and improve your child's understanding of the book they are reading. Hopefully it will mean they get further enjoyment from the book, but, of course, there is always the possibility they might pull in the other direction.

These tasks should have been discussed when you had your original conversation. That way it will come as no surprise to your child when this subject is broached. They should be expecting it.

Basically, in addition to the 15 minutes reading on the last day of the week (obviously you can be flexible with the day if you wish) your child should be given a written exercise to complete in no more than half an hour. Any longer than this and you risk losing all the goodwill you've built up over the last few weeks.

It might be a good idea at this stage to buy an exercise book for your child so they have a brand new book to complete their written work in. Try and explain the importance of presentation at this point as well. (As a teacher, some of the work I am given on a regular basis has absolutely shocking presentation.) It could even become a non-verbal way of communicating with each other: a less threatening way. You can add stickers or put little smiley faces in there for encouragement if you want. But it must become a way of showing that they understand what they are reading.

So, at the end of Week Two, get them to complete the following exercise:

'Read to Understand'

Write a character profile.

Pick one of the major characters in the book and list all of the facts you know about them.

This can start off with a physical description – most authors will spend a bit of time trying to give the reader an image of the main character – then progress onto their family situation and the type of work they are involved with. What hobbies do they take part in (it's normally quite exotic, you don't get many stamp collectors in novels) and where do they spend their leisure time?

Once you have covered the stuff the author has told you then try to work out the things the author has shown you. Remember, you should be able to infer information from clues left in the text. So try and piece together the kind of person that you are reading about. Do they have a temper, or they are quite laid-back and cool about things?

If your child needs a more direct question to answer (some kids might not know where to start with an open-ended task) then ask them, 'What are your impressions of this particular character?' This can then force them to make a much more direct answer to the question.

Anyway get them to write an answer to this question. Don't expect them to produce something in-depth and amazing on their first attempt. Don't get critical of their work – praise their effort – because if they have produced a piece of writing then it does show they are trying to engage with the plan. This will then lead to them becoming more successful through reading.

So remember, about 30 minutes on the writing task is long enough. Not too long so they feel that they are back at school, but long enough to show some kind of commitment.

When they've finished it's time to get ready for Week Three.

WEEK THREE

Firstly, congratulate yourself!

Well done for making it this far. We are almost at the halfway point of the six week reading plan. By now your child may well have finished their first book on this system. If so, well, it's time to order the pizza, break out the Doritos and put the DVD on. Your child should have read 250 pages by this point, and that is certainly not an uncommon length for a piece of teenage fiction.

If the book is complete then you must make sure you celebrate its conclusion properly. Make sure you watch the DVD on a weekend – so you're not rushing them off to bed because it's school in the morning. You could even allow them a day off from their reading, but only if you're convinced it'll start up again the following day. Personally, I'd still make sure the fifteen minutes reading was complete, but I'm prepared to overlook it this once, as long as you promise it's a one-off.

Having this time as a family to celebrate the completion of the book is really vital to your child's engagement with reading. Hopefully you'll enjoy the film, but what you're really after is a bit of feedback from your child about how the book compares with the film. Listen out for comments on the casting of the film, this can prove really effective if your child thinks that one of the main characters looks completely different from how they imagined. Also, chances are that something important will have been left out of the film. Remember that vital learning point I mentioned earlier? It'd be great if your child comments on this – it gives you an opportunity to reinforce the value of reading and how much more detail can be added in a book.

Don't worry if your child hasn't finished their book yet, it may happen next week, or even the week after, just remember to mark the occasion as discussed here.

Once we reach Week Three the chance of disengagement becomes much more unlikely. By now the fifteen minutes reading should have become a habit and your child should be slipping into the act of regularly reading to succeed.

As before, you may feel the need to extend the time slightly or add an extra session in, but only if your child seems to be really responding to the book. Otherwise just maintain the routine and allow your child to slowly work at their own pace.

It's also important to maintain the positive attitude towards reading at this time. Make sure you comment on any news stories that mention Literacy, or any big reading event that is happening around you. If your child appears to want to discuss a book then make sure you grasp the opportunity for them to reflect on what they have read.

You can then set them the task for this week:

'Read to Enquire'

Write a newspaper article about a key event in the book.

Now, I'm assuming that at some point they'll be an exciting or dramatic incident in the book your child is reading. At least I hope so! These events are perfect to mirror the kind of writing you'll find in your daily newspaper.

Children generally like to spend time writing headlines and trying to sensationalise stories. It's the kind of story-telling they are most used to, after all.

Give them a news story you found particularly interesting. It can be from a national or a local newspaper, but try not to make it too daunting by picking a feature length article from The Times. Keep it relatively simple so they can see how it is put together.

They'll need a headline: if they can work in a pun, so much the better. For those of you unsure on puns, they are just a little play on words. I'll give you an example: perhaps an Italian football team didn't do well in their last game – the headline might read, 'Italy Pasta Their Best'. This plays into a couple of stereotypes about Italians, the way they talk and the food they eat. Apologies to any Italian readers out there, but it's exactly the kind of headline a newspaper might use.

Once they have their headline they'll need to put together their first paragraph. When I used to work as a news reporter I remember a sub-editor once telling me that the way to write a report was to imagine your grandmother was reading it. Make it simple and write each paragraph so she could stop whenever she'd had enough. It was good advice.

It's also important to answer as many of the key questions as you can in the opening paragraph:

- Who is the story about?
- What is the story about?
- Where did it happen?
- When did it happen?
- Why did it happen?
- How did it happen?

Have a look at a news story in your newspaper now and see how many of these questions are answered in the first paragraph. I'll wager that most of them are covered in some form or another. So make sure your child is trying to follow that structure. It'd be great if they could add some eye-witness testimony from a character in the book, or even a completely imaginary bystander.

Again, I'd stick to 30 minutes or so for this exercise.

I've often found that kids love to write news stories up onto a computer and design the whole front page. This might not appeal to your kid, but if it does make sure you encourage them to have a go. You never know you might even have something slightly different to pin on your fridge!

WEEK FOUR

Hopefully that bookmark is moving quite rapidly through your child's novel. It may be quite close to the end of a book, or even at the beginning of a new one. Whichever place it's in, as long it's moving forwards and we are seeing some engagement, then – result!

One very anti-reading male student of mine was so badly behaved at home over an extended period of time that he was forced to read, because everything he valued was taken off him as a punishment. Now, I don't condone these methods at all, but the change was quite startling. He came into class and began talking about how he'd read 'Twilight' and other kinds of vampire fiction, but the fact he felt comfortable talking about this in front of his peers was the really amazing thing. Reading was no longer seen as a geeky pastime. Unfortunately this didn't continue once he had won back his gadgets, but hopefully the lesson will stay with him in later life.

This is exactly the kind of attitude that would be great to foster in your child now. Let's cast away these negative ideas of reading as boring or uncool. If more people were to come off the bookshelf and identify themselves as proud readers, perhaps a few more barriers would be demolished. So, if your child can be convinced to read in public they would be championing the cause.

Looking for these kinds of opportunities to read is very important. Chances are that you have some kind of school holiday coming up (as a teacher, I know they come round very quickly at times) and this may involve a holiday somewhere, or a day out. This will obviously involve some kind of journey and reading during travelling is a great way to make the miles go by faster.

One particular journey I remember well is when I took my boys to visit the Warner Brothers Harry Potter Studio Tour (a great trip to reinforce the importance of reading – I know it focuses on the films of the boy wizard, but all of this stemmed from the imagination of a great author). My eldest son had borrowed a book from our school library, passed on by our school librarian – 'A Monster Calls' by Patrick Ness. He read this book throughout the hour and a half drive down to London. We never heard a squeak from him, he was absolutely engrossed. However, as I pulled into the car park, I glanced back to tell the kids we had arrived, only to see tears streaming down his face and hear huge gulps and sobs. My wife and I immediately thought something was wrong, but he just raised his book and said, 'It's this – it's so sad.'

Fortunately he quickly recovered and we had a great day, but it showed the power of literature: how it can hit hard emotionally. I hadn't read the book myself and didn't realise the emotional subject matter it covered. However, it was now top of my reading list. I had to read it myself and see what had so upset him.

So I did – and I sobbed. My wife read it – she sobbed. In fact it has gone through my entire family with the same reaction. It is a beautifully written book and thoroughly recommended. And, no, I'm not going to tell you about the finer details of the plot. No spoilers. Go and read it yourself!

So, if in Week Four you can get the book out of the bedroom, that's great. If you can't – don't worry. As long as your child is reading for the required length of time, let things continue as they are. Don't get frustrated if you're not having any of these defining moments – they'll happen eventually, just keep the faith.

Anyway, now for the next task:

'Read to Empathise'

Imagine you are one of the characters in the book and write a diary entry for them.

This is a critical skill in English, as well as being one that is transferable to other subjects – empathy. It is the skill of putting yourself into the shoes of another person and imaging what life must be like for them. When you think about this it is a skill that will give your child a great deal of tolerance and understanding for the future – what a great world that would be to live in!

You have to be able to write using the language of the character and be able to put yourself in the right mood dependent on the event.

I was undone by this when I first started teaching, and although not wholly relevant to this book, there is a learning point to be had from this.

I was still a student teacher and in charge of a class for the first time. It was an extremely scary moment, having 30 fifteen year old kids staring at me, expecting me to educate them.

However, I had to teach them poetry and tried to engage them with 'Tichborne's Elegy'. This is a great poem written by Chidiock Tichborne on the 19th September 1586. It can be so precisely dated because he wrote the poem on the eve of his execution for treason. He was part of The Babington Plot that tried to overthrow Queen Elizabeth I and replace her on the throne with Mary Queen of Scots. The poem was written to his wife and laments the fact that he is about to lose his life, particularly while he is still so young and with so much to live for.

I asked the kids to imagine they were Chidiock Tichborne, but they had to write a letter, rather than a poem explaining how they felt about their impending execution (I know, it's a bit dark, but I was only learning). One child who was hard to get through to and never offered to share his work thrust up his hand to read out what he had written. Wow, what a moment for a student teacher – had I really got through to such a difficult student?

He composed himself and read out, 'When I die and they lay me to rest, I want to go to the place that's best. When they lay me down to die, I'm going on up to the Spirit in the Sky.'

For those of you not familiar with Dr and The Medics and their classic track, you'll have to Google it. I'm hoping most of you remember this – if so, you'll imagine my embarrassment. I never got the lesson back after that. However, it remains an important lesson for me – that I'll never do that task again, you say? On the contrary, the student showed an understanding of the task and was able to parody it. It might have made for an uncomfortable moment for me, but it showed a great deal of engagement, thought and confidence to pull that off in class.

So, when this is completed, don't be too harsh on your child if they have chosen to try and lampoon the whole task. It actually shows quite a high level of thinking and engagement – just what we're after.

WEEK FIVE

The key issue to guard against now is complacency. Your child has been reading regularly for well over a month and should have finished at least one book. Job done!

But, just like a diet, as soon as you stop putting into practise all the little rules and habits that have built up over this short space of time, you can easily end up back to square one, wondering why you've put all that weight back on.

Now that they are able to 'read to succeed' it should be obvious that reading isn't something that will just happen – it has to be worked on. That's why you need to keep reinforcing those critical messages.

A lot of how you progress will depend on your child. It may be that your kid is a creature of habit and the precise nature of 'same place, same time' works really well for them. Or, they may not enjoy getting into a routine, in which case you have to regularly change the environment they are reading in. You'll have to work with them to ensure the best possible outcome, whatever their preferences.

Hopefully you'll have found the need to 'helicopter' over your child whilst they are reading is now subsiding. Let's face it – you can't stay around them forever, checking on their progress and encouraging them to continue.

Staying on the subject of diets – one of the latest fads is the 5:2 diet. Where you eat what you want for five days and stick to a rigid calorie intake for the other two.

At this stage I still wouldn't recommend loosening the regimental approach we have adopted, but in time your child will probably go through different phases of reading. Just like the 5:2 they may go a couple of days without picking up a book. When this happens it is important not to come down on them too heavily and re-introduce all the measures we have put in place here. As long as you can keep up the correct infrastructure (maintaining your own reading and positive outlook) books will soon make a re-appearance.

So, the task for Week Five:

'Read to Create'

Predict the next section of the novel.

This skill shows you can use the information you have already read to help formulate ideas about what might happen next. The best way of approaching this is to have a go at creating the opening to the next chapter.

This should have the added bonus of helping them develop their creative writing skills. People who read a lot find that they will often mimic the style of their favourite writers. This is not something we should stop them from doing – it's actually a healthy technique. It improves their composition and makes them think about how their sentences should be constructed.

In school we have found that many of our students are losing their ability to create narratives. Writing is critical for your child's future – even if they don't pick up a pen from one week to the next. It is more than likely your child will have to communicate electronically and it is this skill of composition that they often struggle with. Writing allows you to clearly explain things to someone else. How often have mistakes been made because of a lack of clarity? Most issues could have been resolved if the information had been delivered in a clearer fashion.

If your kid struggles with writing short stories get them to look at the opening line of each chapter to see if there is a pattern. Lots of writers have the same tone and structures to their writing and this can be spotted if you look at isolated areas for comparison.

One of the growing areas of creative writing is in 'fan fiction'. This is where readers use minor characters from famous books and write their own stories surrounding them. This is very similar to the task I have just set and, who knows, it may lead your child into an area of writing they find enjoyable.

Perhaps one of the most famous examples of 'fan fiction' is the controversial '50 Shades of Grey', which has taken the publishing world by storm. The author has since made a fortune from the trilogy, which started out as a piece of 'fan fiction' on a Twilight fan site. Hopefully your child won't be writing erotic romance, but if they enjoy developing different elements of a pre-existing title then there are certainly websites they can find to help them showcase their skills.

WEEK SIX

The final week!

Take a little time here to congratulate yourself. Your child has managed to show they can concentrate and read on a regular basis over an extended period of time. And you have helped them achieve this – they now 'read to succeed'.

They may not thank you now, but if you can sustain this impressive start and turn them into a regular reader then there will come a time when they'll be glad you stuck at it.

One of the major criticisms levelled at young people is that they are unable to focus on one thing for an extended period of time. So, by helping them to read on a regular basis you are actually also improving their capacity to concentrate. This is a skill that will prove invaluable as they move towards higher education or the world of work.

When you had the 'conversation' all those weeks ago, you may have agreed a little reward for the successful completion of this programme. Remember to honour any incentive, but don't allow your child to think it's all over. This is just the beginning.

Here is the task for Week 6:

'Read to Communicate'

Write a review of the book you have just read and reflect on the process of reading.

Writing a review is actually a harder skill than it seems. Lots of students want to tell the plot in a very linear fashion, which can be quite dull as well as containing plenty of spoilers. The best way of communicating your thoughts is to give a brief synopsis of the plot, perhaps talk about one particular scene in a little more detail and then give a recommendation and assessment of the book. They can rank the book out of five stars if they wish and it doesn't even matter if they are a little critical of the text – at least it shows they have evaluated the writing at some level.

There should be quite a lot of opportunities to take this piece of work further, if they desire. Lots of schools run magazines that are always crying out for content like book reviews. They can also be posted on websites (such as Amazon) to help other readers decide if the book is something they should be reading.

Reading this book is now helping your child communicate their thoughts and feelings to a much wider audience. Communication is a skill your child probably thinks they are good at, given the amount of social networking that goes on these days. However they need to learn to communicate to different audiences – having a chat with a friend is very different to trying to influence a group of people you don't know.

I have tried to point out different ways in which each of these extra tasks could lead to getting a piece of writing read by a wider audience. It is amazing to see how students react when they actually realise how writing works.

I once got a class of my A Level students to write a newspaper opinion piece about a subject that really annoyed them. Not something they felt a little put out by, but a topic that really got their nexk red.

When they had finished I submitted them to my old editor at the local newspaper and he published them on the letters page in a 'Soapbox' column. The real learning point came when readers of the paper responded to their views. The fact that someone they had never met before, in fact didn't even know of their existence, had taken the time to read their piece, pick up a pen and respond – even if they disagreed with their views – was quite something. The looks on their faces summed up what reading and writing is all about: people being moved emotionally. Sometimes you just don't realise the power a book possesses.

It would be great if you could set your child on the road to becoming a pro-active member of the community by getting them involved in debate, giving them a social conscience as well as improving their writing skills. A regular reader, an entertaining writer and a participating member of the global community – now wouldn't you consider that a success?

CHAPTER SIX:

HAPPILY EVER AFTER

Now that your child has fully engaged with the process of reading it may well feel like the end of a fairy tale. You have been sat there wondering about how to get your child's imagination firing, despairing of them ever showing an interest in reading again and thinking that computer games or social media was going to forever blunt their enquiring minds. Hopefully now you can see that there is a way forward – 'read to succeed'.

But engaging with this process is actually quite different from a fairy tale. For starters there is no bad guy. That is quite a critical message to try and establish early on – no-one is trying to catch anyone out or get them doing something that will have no value. One of the common things you hear often, as a teacher of any subject, is, 'Yes, but when I am going to need to how to do that in real life?'

And, to be fair, they often have a point. However it is the skills you pick up not the content you're exposed to that have the greatest impact as you move through life.

By developing key thinking skills your child will improve their chances to succeed, remember:

SCHEME

UNDERSTAND

COMMUNICATE

CREATE

EMPATHISE

ENQUIRE

DISCOVER

Reading is one of those activities that helps develop skills that are critical in the continual development of your child's future. It is the one thing you literally cannot escape from.

Most children think that English is all about reading Shakespeare and poems. And, grudgingly, I accept that they aren't for everyone. Although I do have to defer to the great film 'Dead Poets Society' here and say:

'We don't read and write poetry because it's cute. We read and write poetry because we are members of the human race. And the human race is filled with passion. And medicine, law, business, engineering, these are noble pursuits and necessary

to sustain life. But poetry, beauty, romance, love, these are what we stay alive for.'

I know, I know. I promised no quotes, but I'm sure you'll forgive me that one.

So, I accept that you are all not going to immediately pick up 'Hamlet' and study the words within. It's all about your children being able to interpret what are reading as they go through life; whether that's a recipe, so they can cook a great meal for their future partner; the small print on their mortgage agreement, so they can become a home-owner; or even 'The Gruffalo', so they can read with their own children when they make you a grandparent. Without practising and building up these skills they lose them. And no-one wants that.

We all want our children to have a 'happily ever after'. I still believe that making them regular readers and helping them 'read to succeed' is the biggest favour you can do for your child.

So don't stop now.

I know how these self-help books work. You follow the programme and everything is hunky-dory for a little while, and then things start to slide, and then things stop, and then you're back to square one.

You and your child have worked hard to get to this point; it would be foolish to stop now.

CHAPTER SEVEN:

THE REVOLUTION

Hopefully the reading habits of your entire family have changed during this process.

I'm praying your whole household now has a positive attitude towards books and reading in general. Remember one of those first rules about not denigrating reading in any way? Well, I'm kind of hoping that you've stuck to that one, particularly considering that you have got this far in the book.

It would be great if you could carry that through and become a convert to the promotion of reading.

It's always said that the most vehement anti-smokers are not those that have never picked a cigarette up in their lives – quite the opposite, it's those who have given up the evil weed and are now reformed. They are the ones who delight in making people feel guilty and want the most draconian laws put in place to stop the disgusting habit. Well let's hope it works like that with you and reading.

In fact, if you feel like trying to be part of the revolution then just sign up right here.

It's all about going back to the preparation work you put in. Remember when you were told to allow yourself to be caught reading? Well, that's what I'm asking of you now. Whether you manage to stuff an old, battered paperback into your pocket, or you have a state of the art e-reader – it doesn't matter – just whip out your reading material at every given opportunity and read.

I'm not talking about skulking in a corner and hiding. I mean stand or sit somewhere prominently and really get yourself noticed. This kind of pro-active reading, this I'm, 'reading and proud of it' attitude is what we need to get reading cool again.

I love actually reading in places where people least expect you to. I mean we can all read while we're waiting for certain things to happen, in the doctor's surgery, at the bus stop, on the train, on holiday, in the garden – and we should certainly continue to do this. But, and I'm really sorry for using this phrase, let's think outside the box a little bit.

Where could you read that might really make a difference?

Lots of people read at half-time during sporting events, but that's mainly newspapers and football programmes. Think about whipping out an Oscar Wilde classic while those around you are scoffing down meat pies and drinking Bovril.

If you read on the park in the sunshine, don't pick a bench out of the way. Why not take your book to the basketball court and read on the sidelines, or on the perimeter of the skate park?

Instead of sitting in the garden, why not head down to the local pub and read there? Lots of people will be socialising and talking, but that's exactly what we're after. And you might feel a little vulnerable, you might get the odd comment, but, again, that's what we need, people to notice that we are reading and proud of it.

We desperately need to stop this 'anti-reading' culture and allowing people easy excuses not to read. Let's make it socially acceptable to 'read to succeed', and let's not worry about being politically correct this once.

We need to shout out, 'Yes, if you don't read, the chances are that I am cleverer than you.'

The whole world needs this reading revolution, so why not be part of it now?

CHAPTER EIGHT: PHONICS

It has been extremely fashionable to teach children to read, during their primary years, by using Phonics. This technique has also become a lot more common in secondary schools as well, which is a sad thing, because it shows how some kids still struggle to identify words when they hit their teenage years.

It certainly works. No question about that. It helps kids to de-code text by connecting a series of sounds together to identify the word. It's actually something I'm sure we can all remember learning, when you mispronounced something and someone sounded the letter out for you, it's not 'cee' it's 'kuh' – a curly 'kuh'.

The only problem we are finding, as kids go through school, is that, with the reluctant readers, they never really get any further than de-coding. The next step is 'understanding' – and that's the important part. I could write something in code now, give you a key and you'd be able to work out what I'd written. It doesn't mean you'd understand it. And that's the key issue I have with Phonics, you need to use these skills as building blocks to regular and consistent reading for meaning.

Now this book is aimed at parents whose kids have fallen out of the habit of reading. It's not really for those kids who can't read or who still struggle to de-code texts. However I think I'd be doing you a dis-service if I didn't at least put in some kind of explanation about how Phonics works. You may have a child who really wants to read widely, but still lacks confidence in some areas and needs a bit of a refresher. If this is the case you will need to know how words are broken up so that you can give your child a bit of help in this regard. So what follows is by no means a comprehensive account of how to use Phonics, but just an introduction so that you can help and, if this turns out to be a key problem, you can look for a more detailed book on how to improve your child's reading.

The system used in UK schools is called 'Synthetic Phonics' and is all about the sounds that combinations of letter make. Now you might think that there'd be 26 sounds, as there are 26 letters of the alphabet. But if you sit and think about it for a minute you'll realise that the letter 'c' sounds different in 'chair' than in 'carrot'. Obviously this is because the letters 'ch' make a different sound.

This is not the only example of different sounds dependent on the positioning of letters. In all there are 44 sounds that can be used to make up words – each of these sounds is called a phoneme.

The best way for me to illustrate this is to firstly give you a list of these sounds. Now, this isn't a talking book, so you're going to have to do this yourself to make it effective. What follows is a list of words: the letters that are printed in bold represent the sound that we're interested in.

For example, the first word is 'SUN'.

This word is helping you identify the 's' sound. It will be written like this: '**S**-UN'.

This is so you can read the word out loud and listen to the sound that is made by that particular phoneme.

Have a go at all 44!

S – **S**-UN

A – **A**-NT

T – **T**-AP

P – **P**-EN

I – **I**-N

N – **N**-ET

M – **M**-AP

D – **D**-OG

G – **G**-O

O – **O**-N

C – **C**-AT

K/CK – SO-**CK**

E – **E**-GG

U – **U**-P

R – **R**-AT

H – **H**-EN

B – **B**-AT

F – **F**-AN

L – **L**-EG

J – **J**-ET

V – **V**-AN

W – **W**-IG

X – MI-**X**

Y – **Y**-ES

Z – **Z**-IP

QU – **QU**-ACK

CH – **CH**-IP

SH – **SH**-OP

TH – **TH**-IN

NG – RI-**NG**

AI – R-**AI**-N

EE – F-**EE**-T

IGH/IE – T-**IE**

OA – B-**OA**-T

OO (short) – B-**OO**-K

OO (long) – M-**OO**-N

AR – F-**AR**-M

OR – B-**OR**-N

UR/ER – F-**ER**-N
OW/OU – **OU**-T
OI – C-**OI**-N
AIR – F-**AIR**
EAR – D-**EAR**
URE – P-**URE**

You can see how these phonemes are used to sound out unfamiliar words. Take the word 'quack' as an example (it is used in the list above).

QU - A - CK

All of the three phonemes in the word can be found on the above list and, if you sound the word out, you can hear every element of the word being pronounced.

Phonics is a useful tool to help kids de-code words and a working knowledge of it is vital, so unfamiliar words can be sounded out in the right way.

As I said, if you want more information, then a quick search on the Internet will give you plenty of food for thought. But right now I'm not going to add to the debate, it's purely here for reference purposes.

CHAPTER NINE:

GUIDED READING

Now guided reading is something you may already think you have done. Your child wasn't reading, but now, through the use of the six week plan in this book, you have guided them to 'read to succeed'. And I can see your point. It does sound as though you have got involved in this.

However, the term 'guided reading' in this sense is a much more educational one. I've included it here, not to look pretentious or clever, but because it is actually a really valuable way of understanding the meaning of books.

I wouldn't use this straight away, or try to employ this tactic to read with your teenage child. But as their love of books develops and they perhaps have to study a book for their GCSE, then this is a technique that is well worth using.

Many people would call for the introduction of 'silent reading' to the classroom. Make sure all kids have fifteen minutes a day where they can read some worthwhile material where you can hear a pin drop. Unfortunately, this kind of whole school approach very rarely works – it certainly didn't for me. When children are forced to read it takes away some of the love and creativity that reading can bring, but, if you don't force them to read, they never read. It's one of the age old 'catch 22' questions.

I remember well the silent reading lessons we had. For starters they weren't silent. A completely quiet classroom is almost viewed as a challenge by certain disruptive types. If they can make a funny noise or draw attention to themselves when the whole room is hushed, then this is obviously well worth the resultant consequence.

Others will remain quiet, but spend the fifteen minutes staring blankly at the same page – not one word making its way from the page through to the brain of the youngster involved. This kind of behaviour is terribly sad. That a child would rather stare at a page than read what's on it is a true indictment of how Literacy, and reading books in particular, is viewed by a lot of children in this country.

I have had children holding their books upside down; some store other material inside so they can read comics under the pretence of analysing a weighty text from the English Canon.

All of this has led me to the conclusion that 'silent reading' in a class full of children is not the answer. It should work when they are on their own with no distractions, but not with all their friends trying to make them laugh.

So, instead of 'silent reading' why not have 'guided reading'.

Basically, in school this involves small groups of children reading to each other, before discussing some of the key themes and issues that arise from the text.

Obviously at home this will look slightly different. You could just start with the two of you, taking it turns to read a few pages and then pose some searching questions on how the book might develop. I'd recommend at this point that you don't pick a book you have already read. It's best to try and explore a new book together here, as kids love to think they are 'on the ground floor' with these kind of projects. Discovering what happens at the same time is a different joy that should always be shared with your children at some point.

When asking questions it's always best to start off with basic comprehension style questions before moving on to the more hypothetical. Start off with some obvious ones about character names and appearances before you get them to stretch their minds in a more difficult direction.

If you can involve other members of the family, then so much the better. You might end up with a veritable book group – and what is wrong with that idea? Absolutely nothing!

I always get my students to find a 'reading buddy' so they can read aloud to each other. This has many benefits. It allows children to practise their pronunciation and become much more adept at reading out loud – a much underrated skill. It gives them the opportunity to discuss certain elements of the book without fear of being belittled. One of the favourite conversations of my Year 13 groups is when they try to cast 'Wuthering Heights'. They all have their own opinions on who would make a good Heathcliff and why. Obviously this is another great opportunity to extol the virtues of a book over a film version, but it also can be an entertaining task – unless, of course, you have no idea who most of the actors are!

'Guided Reading' is used very successfully in schools, if the environment is conducive. It allows the exploration of texts in a peer group setting, often without the direct supervision of teachers, where children can explore ideas and issues that the book raises. This could allow you to talk to your child about some very different topics, or give you new ways to talk about the same old ones.

If you can incorporate this idea into your child's reading time (remember this should be done only when your child becomes very positive about the whole process of reading) then you should find that, as well as increased engagement with reading, there may also be a marked improvement in your relationship. Who'd have thought that books could bring people together like this?

CHAPTER TEN:

WHAT TO READ

I've tried to structure this book in a regular kind of self-help way, but to leave out all the technical features you might find in a book about reading. However, one of the lists you will always come across is a recommended reading list.

Just for this reason I was very tempted to leave it out and point you in the general direction of some of the better books. But it did seem a dereliction of duty. You have bought this book in good faith and are probably expecting some pointers about the specific kind of books your child should be reading.

So for that reason I've overruled myself and included a list of the different kinds of books you might want to try when undertaking the Six Week reading challenge.

Firstly, I want to think of books that fit the criteria of being turned into a film. I made a big song and dance about picking a book that, once read, could then develop into a family pizza and film night. So here is my first list, 'The Top 50 Books Made into Movies This Century'.

My thought process here is to try and pick films that don't look like they were made in the Ice Age. If the film of the book has been released this century, then I figured that it should be a decent enough movie to watch. I have seen the vast majority of these movies and read most of the books too. Some of them are included because they are extremely popular. (For instance, I'll admit to having never read Twilight or seen the film – but enough people have done both and, at its peak, it was a worldwide phenomenon, so it must merit inclusion.)

I could list a short synopsis for each one and recommend reading ages and the like, but the easiest thing to do is to get on Amazon and check them out for yourself. In actual fact this is quite a good task to get your child to help you with before you start the reading process. They should be involved in the selection of the book; going through the plot and checking out the cast in the movie are things that could help with initial engagement. It also gets you talking to each other.

Obviously there are some massive movie franchises that make the list and fill up a few places. Harry Potter takes up seven places on the list – I make no apology for that, they are great books and fantastic movies ('The Order of The Phoenix' is still my all-time personal favourite) that the whole family can enjoy.

Another personal recommendation is 'Holes'. This is a great book with a good adaptation. It was actually the first children's book I read as an adult. I had to teach it to my first ever Year 8 class (a group of students who still hold a special place in my heart) and I loved it – still do. We use Private Peaceful now, which is another great book, but my heart still does mourn the loss of 'Holes'.

In the odd case where the book and film have a different title, I've tried to use the most well-known. However in the case of Philip Pullman's 'Northern Lights' I'm not sure if it is better known by the movie's title 'The Golden Compass'. Either way, you know now.

The Top 50 Books Made into Movies This Century:

Alice In Wonderland – Lewis Carroll

Angus, Thongs and Perfect Snogging –
    Louise Rennison

Beautiful Creatures – Kami Garcia/Margaret Stohl

Because of Winn-Dixie – Kate DiCamillo

The Book Thief – Markus Zusak

Bridge to Terabithia – Katherine Paterson

Charlie and The Chocolate Factory – Roald Dahl

Charlotte's Web – EB White

The Lion, The Witch and The Wardrobe –
    CS Lewis

Prince Caspian – CS Lewis

The Voyage of The Dawn Treader – CS Lewis

Cirque Du Freak – Darren Shan

City of Ember – Jeanne Duprau

Coraline – Neil Gaiman

Diary of a Wimpy Kid – Jeff Kinney

Diary of a Wimpy Kid: Roderick Rules –
    Jeff Kinney

Diary of a Wimpy Kid: Dog Days – Jeff Kinney

Enders Game – Orson Scott Card

Eragon – Christopher Paolini

Fantastic Mr Fox – Roald Dahl

Flipped – Wendelin Van Draanen

Harry Potter and The Philosopher's Stone –
    JK Rowling

Harry Potter and The Chamber of Secrets –
    JK Rowling

Harry Potter and The Prisoner of Azkaban –
    JK Rowling

Harry Potter and The Goblet of Fire –
    JK Rowling

Harry Potter and The Order of The Phoenix –
JK Rowling
Harry Potter and The Half-Blood Prince –
JK Rowling
Harry Potter and The Deathly Hallows –
JK Rowling
The Hobbit – JRR Tolkein
Holes – Louis Sachar
The Hunger Games – Suzanne Collins
Catching Fire – Suzanne Collins
Inkheart – Cornelia Funke
The Invention of Hugo Cabret – Brian Selznick
Madame Doubtfire – Anne Fine
Millions – Frank Cottrell Boyce
Nim's Island – Wendy Orr
Northern Lights – Philip Pullman
Percy Jackson and The Lightning Thief –
Rick Riordan
Private Peaceful – Michael Morpurgo
A Series of Unfortunate Events – Lemony Snicket
Skellig – David Almond
The Spiderwick Chronicles –
T DiTerlizzi and H Black
Stardust – Neil Gaiman
Stormbreaker – Anthony Horowitz
Twilight – Stephanie Meyer
New Moon – Stephanie Meyer
Eclipse – Stephanie Meyer
Breaking Dawn – Stephanie Meyer
War Horse – Michael Morpugo

Of course there are many more great books out there that haven't been made into movies, or have versions that are a little out of date. I'll list another 25 that would work well, but don't just rely on this list – you only have to Google 'Best Teen Reads' and you'll get an endless amount of recommendations 'you must read' just waiting for you to click on.

Obviously you need to check the blurb on these books. Some of them may be more suitable for specific genders; others may have topics you feel are too old for your child. That's fine – censorship is all part of the parental process.

I've not read all of these books. Some were recommended by my students at school, others had good reviews in the newspaper. There are a couple of classics, but most of them are bang up to date.

The Giver – Lois Lowry
City of Bones – Cassandra Clare
Divergent – Veronica Roth
The Fault in Our Stars – John Green
The Perks of Being a Wallflower –
    Stephen Chbosky
Uglies – Scott Westerfield
Vampire Academy – Richelle Mead
Stargirl – Jerry Spinelli
The Angel Experiment – James Patterson
A Monster Calls – Patrick Ness
Lord of The Flies – William Golding
The Curious Incident of the Dog in the Night-Time –
    Mark Haddon
The Graveyard Book – Neil Gaiman
The Lovely Bones – Alice Sebold
In Darkness – Nick Lake
How I Live Now – Meg Rosoff
The Absolutely True Diary of a Part Time Indian –
    Sherman Alexie

Monster – Walter Dean Myers
Where Things Come Back – John Corey Whaley
When You Were Here – Daisy Whitney
Second Chance Summer – Morgan Matson
Beauty Queens – Libby Bray
Shatter Me – Tahereh Mafi
The Raven Boys – Maggie Steifvater
Delirium – Lauren Oliver

CHAPTER ELEVEN:

READING AT SCHOOL

Cards on the table. Gloves off.

Why should you spend time getting your child to read, when, surely, it is the job of the school to educate your little darlings?

To some extent I can sympathise with this viewpoint.

But I want you to understand the reality of school life when it comes to reading.

At Primary School systems like Synthetic Phonics will teach your child to read. At Secondary School their English teachers will endeavour to help them learn how to 'read for meaning'. But very rarely will a school really be set up to encourage your child to 'read to succeed'.

Yes, there are some fantastic school libraries out there, with superb librarians who stock their shelves full of brilliant books and put up posters advertising their services. And they will provide a great resource to those kids who actually read. But we have already established that my book is not designed for parents of those children.

So your child probably never visits that library, possibly would never be seen dead near that library. Your child maybe doesn't engage with that superb librarian, perhaps even thinks that they are a bit sad.

If this is the case then who is actually encouraging your child to read?

Their English teacher will be trying hard. But if the classroom environment is anything like the one I'm used to, then just the mere mention of reading feels like you have broached some taboo subject. Pupils scoff and anyone who might actually read remains quiet for fear of ridicule. Reading is mocked.

The pressure on teachers to ensure their pupils make the required progress is so immense that very few of us have the time to put aside lessons where children can discuss books and the benefits of reading. And the older your child gets, the worse things are.

In my school we run a reading programme and all our younger students get one library lesson a fortnight on their timetable. I hate to bring up that sticky subject of holidays, but school opens for 39 weeks a year – a maximum of 20 hours of library lesson time, unless your child voluntarily frequents the bookshelves.

20 hours is no time at all. Particularly when there is no way they will spend anything like that time reading. When the entire teaching element is taken out: expectations and task-setting and giving things out and collecting things in, there's hardly any time left at all.

In lessons students will be exposed to different extracts of texts, but that doesn't engender a love of reading. For their exams students will be asked to study a particular text (probably 'Of Mice and Men' if your child is taking their GCSE English course) which they may read the whole way through. And that will be about it.

Reading just doesn't get the status it needs in school. OFSTED always bemoan the low Literacy levels that too many youngsters have. But if they walked into a lesson where kids were just sat about reading, I'm sure the teacher concerned wouldn't be receiving an 'outstanding' lesson rating.

Even some of our English A 'Level students don't read that much. I have had students go into an exam without having completely read the set text. And I'm not talking the idle, layabout students here, but normally hard-working, diligent ones.

Reading is just not valued enough in school. All of them pay lip service to it and tell you how important it is, but I've not seen one that truly addresses this issue with their kids in a consistent and effective manner.

So the truth about 'reading for pleasure' in schools is: it just doesn't really happen. That's why we need to change the culture. We need to 'read to succeed'.

That's why it's down to us. If we're going to make a real difference in the lives of our children we need to give them the tools to do it.

'Read to succeed'!

AFTERWORD:

Reading is more important than either wealth or social class as an indicator of success at school. This is a widely established fact. Reading will improve the life chances of your child.

I promised I wouldn't bog down this book with statistics and motivational quotes. But a recent survey by The Institute of Education said that 'Parents are the most important reading role models for children and young people. But only 1 in 5 parents easily find the opportunity to read to their children.'

Does this apply to your family?

Now is the time to act and change the life chances of your child – you owe it to them.

When writing this book I approached it in the same way I teach my students to approach their writing. Think of your purpose and audience.

I guessed that this is the kind of book that you won't want to spend weeks reading. You're probably pressed for time, or might be a reluctant reader yourself. That's fine.

My kids love 'Diary of a Wimpy Kid' and 'Tom Gates' – both of those books weigh in at well under 20,000 words. That was my aim for this book. Make it punchy, make it readable and make it worthwhile.

Hopefully I've achieved this.

Hopefully you are reaping the benefits of extra reading yourself.

Hopefully we will ensure we all 'read to succeed'.

S – Scheme

U – Understand

C – Communicate

C – Create

E – Empathise

E – Enquire

D – Discover

Printed in Great Britain
by Amazon.co.uk, Ltd.,
Marston Gate.